Manifesting Abundance for Witches

Create the Life You Truly Love

Raven Wilder

Contents

What is Manifesting and How Does it Work?

Manifestation has become a popular practice for individuals who want to attract more abundance into their lives. For witches, manifestation can be a powerful tool to bring forth our desires and intentions into reality. Manifestation can help us get the life we truly desire.

Through the use of intention-setting, visualization, spell work, crystals, rituals, and energy work, witches can harness the power of manifestation to create a life filled with abundance. By focusing our thoughts and intentions on what we want to manifest, we can align our energy with the universe and attract the abundance we desire.

By tapping into the energy of the universe and channeling our intentions, witches can bring positive changes to our lives and manifest abundance in all areas, including finances, relationships, and well-being.

Essentially, manifesting involves visualizing and affirming the things that you want to bring into your life, and then taking action towards achieving those goals.

One of the key benefits of manifesting for witches is that it allows us to tap into our innate power and connect with the universe. When you manifest, you are calling upon the universe to bring you the things that you desire and need. This can help you align your energies with those of the universe and create a powerful flow of positive energy that can help to bring abundance into your life.

Manifesting is based on the principle of the law of attraction, which states that like attracts like. This means that the energy and vibrations we put out into the world will attract similar energy and vibrations back to us. By focusing our thoughts and intentions on what we want to manifest, we can align our energy with the universe and attract the abundance we desire.

For example, if you are an optimistic person, you will attract more positive people and situations in your life. If you are a pessimistic person, then you will attract more negative people and situations in your life.

The key to manifestation is not to think about what you do not want, but instead, to think about what you do want. If there is any negative talk in your head that derails you from focusing on something positive, then try thinking of three good things that happen each day.

Let's say that, for example, when you wake up in the morning, you focus on the beautiful sunrise, then you will feel inspired and start your day. If you focus on something you aren't looking forward to, your energy will turn negative, drawing in more negative things into your day.

There is no right or wrong way to manifest abundance.

I am worthy of abundance in all areas of my life

We think of manifesting abundance in terms of money, but the same techniques work for love, joy, health, and fertility. By visualizing our desires as already being present in our lives, witches can send a powerful message to the universe and attract those things into our reality.

Energy work is a key component of manifestation for witches. By aligning our energy with our desires, witches can create a powerful energetic vibration that attracts abundance into our lives. This can involve practices such as meditation, visualization, rituals, or spell work. By working with the energy of the universe, witches can manifest our desires with greater ease and speed.

One of the major benefits of manifesting for witches is the ability to attract abundance in all forms, including financial abundance, which can help us live a more comfortable and fulfilling life. By focusing our intentions on attracting wealth and prosperity, we can open ourselves up to new opportunities and experiences that can lead to financial success.

Witches can also manifest abundance in our relationships and personal lives. By focusing our intentions on attracting loving and supportive partners, friends, and family members, witches can create deeper connections and more fulfilling relationships in our lives.

Besides attracting abundance, manifesting can also help witches cultivate a sense of gratitude and positivity in our lives. By focusing our thoughts and intentions on what we are grateful for and what we want to manifest, we can create a more positive outlook on life and attract even more abundance into our lives.

Another benefit of manifesting is that it can help witches to overcome limiting beliefs and negative thought patterns. Often, we hold ourselves back from achieving our goals because we have negative beliefs and perceptions about ourselves or our abilities. By focusing on our intentions and visualizing ourselves achieving our goals, we can shift our mindset and overcome these limiting beliefs.

Witches have the power to manifest our desires into reality, not only in our personal lives but also in the world around us. Witches can use manifestation to promote social justice and environmental causes. We can manifest positive energy to heal the planet and protect it from negativity. We can also use manifestation to bring justice and peace to a world that desperately needs it. By focusing our energy on these issues, we can help bring about change in the world and make a difference in the lives of others.

Manifesting can be a powerful tool to take control of your destiny and create the life that you want to live. When you focus your energies on your desires and take action toward achieving them, you are taking an active role in shaping your life and creating the future that you want. This can be incredibly empowering for witches as we take control of our lives and carve out our own path.

When it comes to manifesting abundance and success, expecting miracles is a must, but it's important to remember that you have to do the work, too. The law of attraction doesn't exist in isolation. You can visualize all day long but you still need to do things that move you toward your goals. Taking consistent action along with manifesting is a powerful force to help us achieve our dream life.

--•))●((•--

Now, we will cast a spell to bring financial abundance into your life.

Begin by lighting a green candle and holding a piece of citrine in your hand.

Take a deep breath and visualize yourself surrounded by a golden light of abundance and prosperity.

Say the following incantation:

As I light this candle and hold this stone, I call upon the energies of the unknown.

I release any fears or beliefs about lack,

I open myself up to the abundance that I attract.

Money flows to me freely and with ease. I am abundant and prosperous, so mote it be.

Allow the candle to burn down completely and carry the citrine with you as a reminder of your new beliefs and mindset surrounding money. Trust in the universe to provide for you and remain open to the abundance that is coming your way.

So mote it be.

I release any limiting beliefs that block abundance from entering my life

Addressing Your Money Wounds

What happens when our relationship with money is clouded by fear and anxiety? It can be a challenge to navigate the intersection of magic and finances, especially if we carry deep-seated wounds from our past.

Money wounds can be especially difficult for witches to address. We may feel guilty for wanting financial abundance, or we may have inherited beliefs that money is somehow "dirty" or "unspiritual." But the truth is, money is simply a tool that can be used for good or for ill. And as witches, we have the power to use it for good.

Take some time to think about the messages you received about money growing up and the financial decisions you have made as an adult.

Did you see your parents argue about finances or struggle with overspending?

Did you have a parent who struggled with a spending problem?

Were there any negative experiences or beliefs that have been holding you back?

You may find yourself struggling to manage your own finances and you may fear losing the money you have because of things you experienced in your family growing up. These experiences in our childhood can deeply impact our relationship with money as adults.

Once you have a better understanding of your money story, you can make more mindful decisions about money.

Instead of focusing on scarcity and lack, try to focus on abundance and the opportunities that come with it. Celebrate the abundance that you already have in your life, whether it's financial or otherwise. This can help shift your mindset and attract more abundance into your life.

Another helpful practice is to create a budget. This may sound tedious, but it can actually be a liberating experience. By understanding exactly where your money is going, you can make more intentional decisions about how you want to spend it. This can also help ease the anxiety of not knowing where your money is going.

It's important to have a clear idea of what you want to achieve with your money. This can help you stay focused and motivated and can give you a sense of purpose with your finances. Whether it's paying off debt or saving for a big purchase, setting goals can help us stay focused on our financial priorities. Write them down and celebrate each milestone along the way.

Practice mindfulness around money. This can help shift your focus from fear and scarcity to abundance and prosperity. Before making a purchase, take a moment to check in with yourself.

Do you truly need this item?

How will it benefit your life?

By being mindful of our spending habits, we can make more intentional choices with our money.

Take some time every day to express gratitude for the financial abundance you already have in your life. Gratitude can help shift your mindset from scarcity to abundance and can help you attract more abundance into your life.

As witches, we have the power to use money for good and to shape our reality positively. So, embrace abundance and start taking steps toward healing your money wounds today.

Now, focus your attention on your childhood. Think about the messages you received from your family and the wider community about money.

How did your parents talk about money and finances?

Did they view money as something to be feared or something that could bring joy and abundance into their life?

As you reflect on these memories, allow yourself to feel any emotions that come up for you. Acknowledge them and let them pass through you.

Next, shift your focus to the present. Think about the financial decisions you have made as an adult.

What motivated those decisions?

Were they driven by a desire for security or a fear of lack?

As you explore these questions, pay attention to any underlying fears or beliefs about money that might influence your decisions. Are they rooted in scarcity or abundance?

··◦)) ● ((◦··

Visualize a clear, flowing stream of money coming toward you, flowing into your life with ease and grace. See yourself surrounded by abundance and prosperity, and feel the joy and freedom that comes with it.

Repeat the following three times:

"Money flows to me with ease and grace, abundance and prosperity in this space. I release any fears or beliefs that hold me back, and welcome the prosperity that I now attract."

As you repeat these words, feel the power and energy behind them.

Believe that you are worthy of financial abundance and that it is already on its way to you.

Know that you have the power to manifest abundance and prosperity in your life and that you can always return to this visualization whenever you need to realign your energy with the flow of money.

How does that make you feel?

Are you feeling anxious about money coming to you?

What is the underlying cause of this anxiety? Is it rooted in a belief you formed in childhood or an insecurity that has been reinforced as an adult?

Take the time to really get to know these underlying causes. Acknowledge and accept them.

Notice any emotions that come up for you as you reflect on these messages.

Do you feel guilty for not being able to make ends meet? Are you ashamed of not having enough money in savings?

Is your fear rooted in a lack of knowledge or an underlying belief that money is scarce?

Is it something else? Take a few seconds to really consider this question.

These feelings are normal. Be gentle with yourself.

Picture yourself surrounded by a golden light that brings you safety and security. Imagine this light soothing away any negativity or fear you may have about money, allowing you to accept and embrace the positive potential of money and the possibilities it can provide.

Remember, you are capable of taking control of your finances and creating a life that you can be proud of. Anything is possible.

You are capable.

You are strong.

Now let go of thoughts and worries and just be.

The following spell will guide you in reflecting on the messages you received about money while growing up and the impact the messages have had on your financial decisions as an adult. You can use a green candle to represent money or any color that speaks to you.

··•)〉●《(•··

Goddess of financial abundance, I call upon thee.

As I light this candle, I ask for your guidance on my financial journey.

As I reflect on my past, I recognize the messages I received about money from my family and community.

I release any negative beliefs and emotions that may be hindering my financial growth.

I call upon the power of manifestation to attract wealth and abundance into my life.

I affirm that money flows to me easily and effortlessly.

I release any fears or limiting beliefs that may hold me back from achieving financial success.

I trust in the universe to provide me with all the resources I need to thrive.

I ask for your help in making wise financial decisions that align with my highest good.

May love, abundance, and generosity guide my actions.

I am grateful for the financial blessings that are coming my way. I trust in your divine plan and surrender to the flow of abundance.

Thank you, goddess of financial abundance, for your love and support.

So mote it be.

Remember, healing takes time, but you have the power to move past the challenges of your family's past and create a bright financial future for yourself. Healing from money wounds can be a long and difficult journey, but you don't have to do it alone. Seek support from friends, family, a therapist, or a financial planner who can help you work through your challenges and provide accountability as you work toward your goals.

I trust that the universe will provide me with everything I need

Clear Money Blocks and Limiting Beliefs

Many of us have dreams of having more success, wealth, love, and happiness. As witches, we are no exception. We are always looking to manifest our desires and live our lives to the fullest. However, often the things holding us back are our own mental obstacles.

We might not even realize it, but our subconscious beliefs and fears can sabotage our efforts to achieve our goals. If you're feeling stuck and unable to move forward, it's likely because you're subconsciously holding yourself back. But don't worry, there are ways to overcome these obstacles and step into your power.

One thing that holds us back is keeping ourselves small so that others don't feel less than us. As witches, we are often very empathetic and compassionate toward others. We want to make sure that everyone around us feels good about themselves. However, this can sometimes lead us to play small and hold back our own achievements and success. It's important to remember that we are not responsible for how others feel about themselves. We can inspire and uplift others, but ultimately, our own self-worth and confidence comes from within. We should never dim our own light to make others feel more comfortable.

We may also believe that we are not worthy of success or that we are not capable of achieving our goals. These beliefs are often rooted in our past experiences or the stories we tell ourselves. We can be stuck in the belief that we don't deserve abundance and success. This can lead to feelings of worthlessness and can keep us from taking the steps necessary to create a life of abundance.

Feeling like you don't deserve to live an abundant life can be a huge barrier. It's important to remember that you deserve to have a life of abundance. We all have gifts and talents and we can create a life of abundance for ourselves.

You just have to believe it and take action.

You are worthy of success.

As witches, we have the power to rewrite our stories and change our beliefs. We can use spells, affirmations, and visualization techniques to shift our mindset and overcome our limiting beliefs.

Negative people in your life can also hold you back from living a life of abundance. Whether it's family, friends, or partners, it's important to be mindful of the people in our lives and how our beliefs and attitudes can affect us.

If someone is constantly putting you down and discouraging you, it's important to take a step back and reevaluate the relationship. If we're surrounded by the right people, success shouldn't be a threat to these relationships.

If you are nervous about sharing your successes with someone in your life, that can be a sign that this person isn't healthy for us. Success should bring us closer to the people we love, as it allows us to share our joy and successes with them. If we're surrounded by the right people, success shouldn't be a threat to these relationships. It's important to remember that success can bring us closer to the people we love and that it can open doors to a more abundant life.

Another mental obstacle that can hold us back is the fear of failure. We can sometimes put too much pressure on ourselves to always get things right. We might be afraid to take risks or try new things because we fear we will fail and our manifestation powers will be proven to be ineffective. It's important to remember that failure is not something to be feared. In fact, it's often a necessary step toward success. Every successful person has experienced failure at some point in their journey. Instead of fearing failure, we should embrace it as an opportunity to learn and grow.

Another mental obstacle that can hold us back is the fear of rejection. As witches, we are often very intuitive and sensitive to energy. We might fear that if we put ourselves out there and ask for what we want, we will be rejected or face negative energy. This fear can keep us from taking risks and going after our dreams. It's important to remember that rejection is not a reflection of our worth or value. It's simply a part of life. We should never let the fear of rejection hold us back from going after what we want.

So, how can we overcome these mental obstacles and step into our power as witches?

We need to identify our limiting beliefs and fears.

What are the stories we tell ourselves about our abilities and potential?

What are the things we're afraid of?

Once we identify these things, we can work to reframe them and change our beliefs to be more supportive of our goals.

It's important to surround ourselves with like-minded individuals who support and encourage us on our journey. We can seek out witches who are also on the path to success and abundance and learn from them. Joining or attending events where we can connect with other witches can help us build a support system. Join our Facebook group, Manifesting Abundance for Wtiches to find a community of like-minded witches.

We need to surround ourselves with supportive people who uplift and inspire us. Mentors, friends, and community members who believe in us and our potential are important. We should also be willing to give support to others and be a positive influence in our lives.

We need to take action toward our goals, even if it feels scary or uncomfortable. We need to step out of our comfort zones and take risks.

When living a life of abundance, it's important to take calculated risks.

While it is natural to feel anxious about investing and taking chances, it's important to remember that the rewards can often outweigh the risks. We might not always succeed, but every step we take toward our goals is a step in the right direction.

There are so many misconceptions out there about wealth and abundance, which can lead to feelings of guilt or shame. But it's important to remember that wealth is not a bad thing and that it can be a positive force in our lives and in the lives of our loved ones. We've all been influenced by stereotypes of "rich people" that can make us shy away from creating a life of abundance. There are many successful people out there who are generous and kind.

If you're feeling stuck, take a step back and eval-
uate what may be holding you back. With a little
bit of self-reflection and a lot of determination, you
can create the life of abundance you desire. With
a positive attitude and the right mindset, you can
achieve your dreams and live a life of abundance.

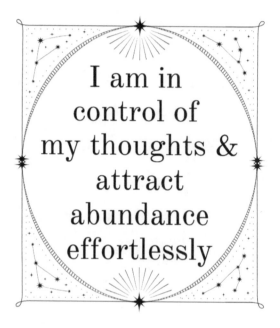

I am in control of my thoughts & attract abundance effortlessly

Clearing Resistance to Being Successful

Resistance to living an abundant life can arise from within us, from our old beliefs, from our subconscious, or from outside sources. It can take many forms, such as fear, worry, guilt, and shame. It's important to recognize and address the resistance that's blocking you from the life you desire.

We all want to be successful. But sometimes our minds and emotions can be the biggest obstacles that stop us from achieving our goals. We may feel stuck, fearful, or overwhelmed.

In order to clear these blocks and move forward, it's important to take steps to release resistance. Doing this work is necessary in order
to move forward in an abundant life. There are
many ways to clear resistance and create space
to build an abundant life.

Meditation can help you get in touch with your
inner beliefs and clear out any negative energy.
It can be especially helpful to practice guided
meditations that focus on abundance and success. Meditation is a great way to calm and focus
your mind, allowing you to connect with a higher
power and receive guidance. It can help you clear
away any mental blocks that are preventing you
from achieving abundance.

Tapping, also known as Emotional Freedom
Technique (EFT), is a form of energy therapy that
helps to clear blocks from the energy fields surrounding your body. It's a powerful tool for releasing resistance and allowing abundance to flow,
releasing emotional blocks and negative energy.
EFT is a technique that involves tapping your body
on certain body parts in order to release tension
and stress. Tapping can help you let go of any neg-

ative emotions and align yourself with your goal of abundance.

Taking a ritual bath with herbs like rosemary, ginger, jasmine, or lavender can be a powerful way to cleanse yourself and your surroundings, clear away negative energy, and create space for abundance.

Clearing negative energy from your home is essential for creating a space that's conducive to success. Techniques such as smudging with sage, using crystals, and other rituals can help to do this. Burning sage or palo santo wood is a great way to cleanse and refresh your space. Crystals can help to raise the vibration of your home, allowing for positive energy to flow freely.

Say 'I love money' repeatedly until you can say it without feeling uncomfortable. This may sound like a strange thing to say, but loving money can make us feel uncomfortable. By saying it over and over, we desensitize ourselves to the word and become comfortable with the idea of loving money.

I am letting go of fear and doubt and trusting in the universe to guide me towards my desires

You deserve safety, security, and abundance.

You deserve safety and security and money can bring that to you.

You deserve to live your life with confidence and purpose.

You are capable of achieving your goals.

You are capable of creating the life of abundance that you desire.

Allow yourself to take the steps necessary to make this a reality.

When we free ourselves from the blocks and resistance that are holding us back, we can create a life of abundance that's just waiting to be unlocked.

A meditation script to clear resistance for a successful and abundant life.

Make yourself comfortable in a seated position, close your eyes, and take a few deep breaths, in and out.

Feel the tension in your body dissolve away as you focus on your breath. Allow yourself to become more relaxed. Visualize yourself in a space of abundance and success.

Now, imagine a beautiful, sunny day. Feel the warmth of the sun on your skin, and allow the feeling of contentment to wash over your body.

Now, imagine yourself in a place of complete abundance, where all of your dreams are coming true.

You feel empowered and successful. An energy of positivity and joy surrounds you.

As you sit in this place, notice any resistance or doubts that arise in your mind.

Allow yourself to simply observe these thoughts and feelings without judgment.

Now, imagine a light of love and compassion surrounding and enveloping these thoughts and feelings. Imagine the light transforming any resistance and doubts into feelings of acceptance and possibility.

Feel the joy and excitement that comes with living a life you love. Feel the strength and courage you have to achieve your goals and dreams. Any resistance you feel is dissipating away, leaving you open up to a successful and abundant life.

Allow yourself to be filled with gratitude for all that you have achieved and all that is to come. Feel the confidence and the trust in yourself that you can create the life you desire. Take a few moments to really savor this feeling.

Now, take a few deep breaths and notice any shifts in your body and mind. Imagine yourself embodying the energy of success and abundance and feeling free to create a life of joy and abundance.

Now let yourself return to a state of relaxation. Let go of thoughts and worries and just be.

When you are ready, slowly open your eyes. Come back to the present moment. Take a few more deep breaths and give yourself permission to be successful and live an abundant life.

Overcome a Fear of Being Seen

Witches have been persecuted for centuries, accused of practicing dark magic and being in league with the devil. These accusations have led to countless witch hunts and trials, resulting in the deaths of many innocent people.

Although we live in modern times, the history of witch persecution can still make modern practitioners nervous about being seen. This fear of persecution can lead to a struggle with manifesting the abundant life that you deserve.

The history of witch persecution dates back to ancient times. In many cultures, witches were revered for their spiritual wisdom and healing abilities. However, as Christianity swept through Europe, the Church began to view witchcraft as a heretical practice that threatened the power of the Church. Witch hunts began in the late medieval period and continued until the 18th century. During this time, thousands of people, mostly women, were accused of witchcraft and were executed for our alleged crimes.

The Salem Witch Trials in the late 17th century were one of the most infamous examples of witch persecution in history. Accusations of witchcraft in Salem sparked a wave of hysteria that led to the execution of 20 people. Innocent people were accused and convicted based on flimsy evidence.

The witch hunts were fueled by a fear of the unknown, fear, superstition, and a desire to control those who were different. Those accused of witchcraft were often tortured until they confessed, and their confessions were often obtained through coercion or manipulation. Many of the accusations were based on rumors and hearsay, with little or no evidence to support them.

Despite the fact that witch hunts are a thing of the past, the fear of being seen as a witch still lingers in modern times. While witchcraft is no longer illegal, many people still view it as a dark and dangerous practice, associating it with evil and harm. This perception is fueled by sensationalized media portrayals and a lack of understanding about what witchcraft really entails. Negative stereotypes are perpetuated by popular culture, which portrays witches as evil and malevolent beings who seek to harm others.

Modern practitioners of witchcraft may struggle with the fear of being judged or misunderstood by others, even in communities that are generally accepting of alternative spiritual practices. This fear can be especially pronounced for those who live in politically or religiously conservative communities, where witchcraft is often viewed with suspicion or outright hostility.

Witches who are afraid of being seen may struggle with expressing their true selves. They may fear being judged or ostracized by society. This fear can lead to a lack of self-confidence and can prevent witches from fully embracing their spiritual power.

This fear can have a profound impact on our ability to manifest the abundant life we deserve.

When we are constantly worried about what others think of us, we are unable to fully embrace our power and tap into the magic that lies within us. Instead, we may find ourselves holding back, second-guessing ourselves, and ultimately, limiting our potential.

The fear of persecution can also lead to a lack of trust in the universe. Witches who are afraid of being seen may struggle with manifesting their desires because they do not trust that the universe will support them. This lack of trust can create a self-fulfilling prophecy and can prevent witches from living the abundant life they deserve.

To overcome the fear of being seen, it is important for witches to embrace our unique gifts and talents. We must believe in ourselves and trust that the universe will support us. By embracing our true selves and trusting in the universe, we can manifest the abundant life we deserve.

One way to overcome the fear of being is to connect with other witches. By building a community of like-minded individuals, witches can find support and encouragement. This community can provide a safe space for witches to express themselves freely and without fear of judgment. Visit our Facebook group, Manifesting Abundance for Witches to connect with other witches who are on the same path to abundance.

Another way to overcome these struggles is to embrace the positive aspects of witchcraft and focus on the abundance that it can bring. Witchcraft is a practice that emphasizes personal empowerment, self-care, and the use of natural resources to create positive change in the world. By embracing these core principles, modern practitioners of witchcraft can begin to see themselves as deserving of abundance and success. We can also begin to cultivate a sense of confidence and self-worth that will help us to overcome our fears and pursue our goals with greater ease and clarity.

Ultimately, overcoming the fear of being seen requires us to embrace our true selves and stand in our power. We must recognize that our beliefs and practices are valid, important and that we have the right to live our lives authentically and without fear of judgment or persecution.

In doing so, we can tap into the abundance and magic that lies within us, manifesting the life we truly deserve. We can harness our intuition and connect with nature, finding peace and harmony in the world around us. And we can inspire others to embrace our own power and magic, helping to break down the barriers of fear and misunderstanding that still exist.

I believe in
my power to
manifest
abundance
in my life

Intuition

It's important to tap into your intuition to manifest abundance. Your intuition is a powerful tool that can guide you toward the path of abundance and fulfillment. As witches, we have the power to use our intuition and connection to the universe to make it happen. Whether it's a beautiful house, a successful business, a loving relationship, or enough money to live comfortably, abundance has the power to unlock a world of possibilities. It's crucial to tap into this inner wisdom and trust the insights it provides.

Take a moment to reflect on what your intuition is telling you about manifesting abundance.

What goals will make you content and fulfilled if you achieve them?

What goals are truly important to you?

What will make you feel content and fulfilled if you achieve them?

Your intuition may tell you that you're not on the right path or that there's something blocking you from manifesting the abundance you desire.

Sometimes, we get caught up in the pursuit of external success and forget to listen to what our intuition is telling us about what truly matters.

Jealousy can be an uncomfortable emotion, but it can also be a sign of what you truly want. Instead of suppressing it or pushing it away, take a moment to reflect and try to uncover what your intuition is telling you.

Are you jealous of someone else's success because it's something you truly desire for yourself? If so, let that jealousy guide you toward your own path to success.

Resistance can also be a sign that something isn't aligned with your intuition. If you're feeling resistance to taking action toward your goals, it's important to explore why. Is there something holding you back?

Are you afraid of failure or success?

When you feel resistance or fear, take a step back and figure out what is causing it.

Are you aiming for something because you believe you should, or because it is truly something you desire?

Where you are putting your focus is incredibly important.

Are you constantly worrying about the potential of something negative happening? Or are you placing your focus on what you really want and on your goals?

If you're feeling overwhelmed by potential negative things that could happen, try to shift your focus to what you want and your goals. By doing so, you'll be sending a powerful signal to the universe which will help to manifest abundance in your life.

Remember, where you put your focus is what will happen.

Are you focused on potential things you want to happen or negative things that could happen?

Are you putting your focus on what you want and your goals?

Is there something you really want to manifest? Put your focus on it and watch the miracles in your life unfold.

Your intuition can guide you toward understanding these blocks and help you overcome them. Remember to listen to your intuition and trust the insights it provides. By doing so, you'll be able to manifest the abundance and success you desire and live a fulfilling life aligned with your truest desires.

The first step to manifesting abundance is to be open to the idea. Open your mind to the possibility of abundance and create space for it to flow into your life.

Take a few deep breaths.

Allow yourself to become open to the idea of abundance.

Find a comfortable spot to sit and close your eyes. Take a few more deep breaths and let your body relax.

Now, imagine a bright white light entering your body. Feel the light radiating from your core and expanding throughout your body. This light is your intuition, and it is guiding you to unlock your potential and manifest abundance.

Focus on this light and allow it to fill your entire being. Take a few moments to connect with this light and feel its warmth and power.

Now, imagine the abundance you desire.

Joy.

Financial abundance.

Fulfillment.

Love.

Whatever it is, visualize it and focus on the feeling of having that abundance in your life. Allow yourself to feel the joy and gratitude of having that abundance and know that it is possible.

Now, ask your intuition to guide you. Ask it to show you what steps you need to take to manifest abundance in your life.

Take a few moments to listen. Be open to whatever comes to you.

Now, take some time to envision your wildest dreams and desires.

Feel the emotion and excitement of having abundance in your life.

Allow yourself to be receptive to this energy.

Now, bring your focus to your heart center. Feel the powerful energy of your intuition and the guidance it can provide.

Listen to the wisdom of your heart and trust in its guidance. As you continue to relax into the energy of your meditation, imagine a brilliant, golden light expanding out from your heart center and filling your entire body.

The energy of abundance will open the doors to manifesting your desires. Take a few moments to visualize your desired outcome.

See yourself living a life of abundance.

See yourself happy, healthy, and surrounded by all the abundance you desire.

Allow yourself to feel the joy and gratitude of having these things in your life.

Let your intuition guide you and trust that it will lead you to the right path.

Now let yourself return to a state of relaxation. Let go of thoughts and worries and just be.

When you're ready, slowly open your eyes. Take a few moments to reflect on the insight you've gained and the abundance that awaits you.

···•))●((•···

Now that your mind is clear and focused, here is a spell to help you tap into your intuition.

Gather the following items:

- A purple candle
- A clear quartz crystal
- A piece of amethyst
- A piece of labradorite
- A small bowl of salt
- A pen and paper

Begin by finding a quiet and comfortable space where you can perform the spell without interruption.

Light the purple candle and place it in front of you.

Take a few deep breaths, allowing yourself to relax and clear your mind.

Hold the clear quartz crystal in your left hand and the amethyst in your right hand.

Say the following: "Crystal clear and shining bright, Guide me now with inner sight. Open pathways to intuition's flow, Let my guidance effortlessly show."

As you speak these words, imagine the crystals glowing brightly and filling your body with our energy.

Close your eyes and visualize a bright light surrounding you, enveloping you in a protective shield. This light is your connection to the divine, and it will guide you as you tap into your intuition.

Now repeat this affirmation: "May my intuition be clear and strong, May guidance come to me all day long. With this spell, I call upon my inner sight, To lead me true and guide me right."

Next, take the piece of labradorite and place it on the piece of paper. Using the pen, write any questions or concerns that you have been struggling with. These can be related to any aspect of your life, such as relationships, career, or personal growth.

Once you have written your questions, place the paper with the labradorite on top of the small bowl of salt. The salt will help to purify and cleanse the energy surrounding your questions, making it easier for you to access your intuition.

Hold your hands over the paper and salt, and focus your energy on your questions.

Allow yourself to be open to whatever insights or guidance come to you.

You may feel a tingling sensation in your hands or a sense of warmth spreading throughout your body.

Trust that these are signs that your intuition is opening up and guiding you.

After a few minutes, pick up the labradorite and hold it in your hands.

Close your eyes and allow your intuition to guide you as you meditate on your questions.

You may receive insights or messages in the form of images, words, or feelings.

Trust that whatever comes to you is exactly what you need to hear at this moment.

When you feel ready, take the piece of paper with your questions and burn it using the flame of the purple candle. As you watch the paper burn, visualize your questions being released into the universe, and trust that the answers will come to you in your own time.

Finally, hold the clear quartz crystal in your hands and thank the divine for guiding you and helping you tap deeply into your intuition.

Place the crystal on your altar or in a special place where you can see it and be reminded of your connection to your intuition.

I trust the journey of my manifestations and know that everything is working out for my highest good

Clarifying your Intentions

As a witch, you have a unique perspective on abundance and the power of manifestation. You understand that abundance is not just about material wealth, but also about the energy and intention that you bring to your life.

For witches, the power of manifesting is a fundamental practice in our craft. It involves harnessing the energy of the universe and directing it toward your goals, desires, and intentions.

However, without a clear understanding of what you truly want, your manifestations may not yield the desired results.

So, what does an abundant life mean to you?

Perhaps it means having the resources to practice your craft in the way that feels most authentic to you.

Maybe it means having the time and space to connect with nature and the divine.

Or perhaps it means being able to share your gifts and talents with the world in a way that uplifts and inspires others.

An important step in clarifying your intentions is to get specific about what you want.

Instead of vague statements like "I want more money," be specific about how much money you want and what you want to do with it. For example, "I want to earn $10,000 by the end of the year to pay off my debt and take a trip to Europe." The more specific you are, the easier it is for the universe to understand what you want and deliver it to you.

Manifesting is not just about thinking positively; it's about feeling positive emotions that align with your desires. When you think about your intentions, pay attention to how you feel. If you feel excited, happy, and grateful, you're on the right track. If you feel doubtful, anxious, or scared, it's a sign that you need to clarify your intentions further or work on blocks that may be holding you back.

Visualization is a powerful tool for manifesting. When you visualize your desires, you create a mental picture of what you want to manifest. It helps you get clear about your intentions and connects you to the emotional energy of your desires.

Close your eyes and imagine yourself experiencing your desires as if they have already come true.

What do you see, hear, and feel?

The more vivid your visualization, the more powerful your manifestation will be.

Writing your intentions is another powerful way to clarify them. When you write down your intentions, you give them a physical form, making them more tangible and real.

Write your intentions in the present tense as if they have already come true. For example, "I am happy and grateful for the $10,000 that I have earned by the end of the year."

Keep your written intentions somewhere you can see them every day, like on your vision board or in your journal.

Clarifying your intentions is essential for effective manifesting. By getting specific, tapping into your emotions, visualizing your desires, writing them down, and trusting the universe, you can use the power of manifesting to get what you truly want in your life. Remember to stay positive, trust the process, and have fun with your manifesting practice!

When you have abundance, you can invest in yourself and those around you.

You can take risks without worrying about the financial repercussions.

Having financial security is not just about being able to buy nice things, it's also about having the means to do good.

It's about finding the right mix of financial resources, time, and energy to make the most of life. It's about having the means to do good in the world, while still indulging in the things that bring you joy.

So, what do you want out of life?

What is your definition of abundance?

Consider these questions and think about what your goals are and why you want to manifest abundance in your life.

Once you have set your intentions, let go of any attachment to the outcome. Trust that the universe will deliver what is best for you, even if it's not exactly what you had in mind.

Remember that the universe works in mysterious ways and may have something even better in store for you.

···)) ● ((···

Meditation to clarify your intentions.

Take a few moments for yourself to reflect and meditate on the question, "What do I want out of life?" using this meditation script. Find a comfortable spot to sit and close your eyes. Take a few deep breaths and notice how your body is feeling.

Now, take a moment to listen to the sound of your breath, the rhythm of the air entering and leaving your lungs. Let this become the main focus of your awareness.

Once you feel settled, bring your attention to the question "What do I want out of life?".

Now, breathe in and as you exhale, allow yourself to silently repeat the question, "What do I want out of life?".

Pay attention to any sensations, thoughts, images, or words that come up. Take your time and explore what arises, without judgment. Once you've had some time to reflect, take a few more deep breaths and slowly open your eyes.

When you're ready, take a few moments to jot down any insights that have come up for you during the meditation. Remember, this meditation is just the beginning of a beautiful journey of self-discovery. You don't have to have all the answers right away. Take it one step at a time and trust that you'll be guided to where you need to go.

Create an Altar for Abundance

C reating an altar in your home is a great way to draw abundance and manifest the desires of your heart. Whether it's a career goal, a financial wish, or simply a desire to bring something new and wonderful into your life, an altar can be an incredibly powerful and effective tool.

When creating an altar, think about the energy of abundance and how you want to feel when you look upon it. Choose a space in your home that feels sacred and special to you. It can be a corner of your bedroom, a shelf in the living room, or even an entire room dedicated to your spiritual practice.

Once you have your space, you can decorate it with meaningful objects that reflect your intentions. Include candles, stones, crystals, incense, coins, jewelry, images of your dreams and goals, flowers, and other meaningful items that bring to mind the idea of abundance and can all be used to create an altar that is uniquely yours.

You can incorporate symbols, elements, and items that represent the feelings you want to experience.

Lighting candles is a common way to create a sacred or special space. Choose candles you enjoy, feel a connection with, and that reflect your intentions for your altar. You can also choose to use candles with special meanings or that represent your core values.

Crystals are often used to bring positive energy and healing into a space. Choose crystals that are associated with abundance and wealth, such as citrine and green aventurine.

Symbols can be a powerful way to invoke a certain emotion or feeling. Choose symbols that represent wealth, prosperity, and abundance. Consider using coins, shells, feathers, trees, and prosperity symbols.

Choose images of things that you want to bring into your life, such as a house, a car, or a dream vacation. You can write a check to yourself for the amount of money you want to manifest, give yourself a certificate of achievement, or even a marriage certificate to draw a mate into your life.

Rituals can be a fun and creative way to bring your altar to life. Take a few moments each day to sit before your altar, light a candle, and say a few words of gratitude for the abundance that is already in your life. You can also use your altar for smudging, meditating, or other spiritual practices.

You can also add a personal touch to your altar by writing your intentions for a more abundant life. Be specific about what you want to manifest and use positive affirmations to help bring it into being.

When you're ready to work with your altar, start by lighting a candle and taking a few moments to clear your mind and focus on your intentions.

Once your altar is set up, take some time each day to visit it.

Spend a few moments in reflection on what you want to manifest and allow yourself to be present with your thoughts and feelings. Light a candle and spend a few minutes of quiet time in reflection.

You can also turn your wallet into an abundance altar.

A few simple steps can help you create a powerful tool to open yourself up to receiving abundance so that you can share it with the world.

Take everything out of your wallet. Clear your wallet of old receipts, business cards, and clutter. Clearing out your wallet, you're making room for the energetic pathways of abundance to flow. Allowing these pathways to carry the energy of abundance is the key to attracting more of the things that you want in your life. The more clutter that's in the way, the harder it is for this energy to get to you. Take a few moments to go through your wallet and clear out anything that's unnecessary. Toss out old receipts, business cards, and any other items you don't need.

Smudge your wallet. This helps clear out any stagnant energy that may prevent abundance from entering your life.

Only return the items that are absolutely necessary and useful.

Hold your wallet and set an intention. "I am open to receiving abundance."

You may also place meaningful items such as small crystals, a silver dollar, paper money that you do not spend, or an abundance spell in your wallet.

Choose items that have meaning for you and other items you think will help your altar work its magic.

··•)) ● ((•··

By creating an altar, you can enhance your manifestation abilities by creating a physical representation of your desires. Your altar serves as a reminder to stay focused and committed to your goals. The act of regularly visiting and adding to the altar can help to reinforce your intentions and keep them at the forefront of your mind.

An altar can be a powerful tool for us to enhance our manifestation abilities and bring abundance into our lives. By creating a sacred space and setting clear intentions, we can tap inner our inner power and manifest our dreams into reality.

An Abundance Vision Board

S ometimes, it's difficult to keep our desires at the forefront of our minds amidst the chaos of everyday life. This is where a vision board can come in handy. A vision board is a powerful tool that can help us to manifest our dreams. A vision board is a visual representation of our goals, dreams, and desires that we can create to help us focus our energy and bring our intentions to fruition.

Before you create your vision board, take some time to get clear on what you truly desire. This can be anything from a new job to a loving relationship to financial abundance. Write your intentions as specific as possible. The more clarity you have, the more powerful your manifestation will be.

Once you have a clear idea of what you want to manifest, it's time to choose images and words for your vision board. Look for pictures and phrases that resonate with you, and that evoke feelings of joy, abundance, and success. You can also include symbols that represent your desires, such as a dollar sign for financial abundance or a heart for love.

A vision board can be a physical or digital collage of images, words, and symbols that represent your intentions and desires. It can be created using a variety of materials, including magazines, photos, stickers, and other decorative items. Some witches prefer to create a digital version using Pinterest or other online tools, while others enjoy the tactile experience of cutting out images and words from magazines and gluing them onto a poster board.

The key is to choose images and symbols that resonate with you and represent what you want to manifest in your life.

I am deserving
of love and a
fulfilling
relationship

For example, if you are hoping to manifest a new job, you might include images of a specific company you'd like to work for, or photos of people in your desired field doing work that you find inspiring.

Once you have gathered your materials and chosen your images, it's time to create your vision board.

Before you place your images and words on your vision board, take some time to set your intentions with a ritual. This can be as simple as lighting a candle and stating your intentions out loud, or as elaborate as a full moon ritual. Whatever feels right for you, do it with intention and focus.

Start by meditating or grounding yourself in order to connect with your intuition and set your intentions.

Then, begin arranging your images and symbols on your board in a way that feels meaningful and powerful to you.

Group your images by theme or intention, or create a more abstract representation of your desires.

Once your vision board is complete, it's time to work with it to manifest your desires. Place it in a prominent place where you will see it every day. This could be your bedroom, your office, or even your altar. The more you see your vision board, the more it will remind you of your intentions, and the more energy you will put toward manifesting them. I made a digital vision board and set it as the home screen of my computer. I see my vision board multiple times a day as I work toward my goals throughout the day.

Spend time each day focusing on your vision board and visualizing yourself already having achieved your goals and desires. Meditate on specific images or symbols on your board, or simply look at your vision board and allow yourself to feel the emotions of having already achieved what you desire.

Every time you look at your vision board, take a moment to visualize yourself already in possession of the things you've included in it. Imagine how it feels to have that job, that new relationship, or that dream home. The more you can tap into the feeling of already having what you desire, the more likely it is to manifest in your reality.

Use your vision board as a tool for setting and achieving specific goals. You can break down your larger desires into smaller, actionable steps, and then create action plans based on those steps.

For example, if your desire is to start your own business, you might break that down into smaller goals, such as creating a business plan, identifying potential customers, and setting up a website.

You can then use your vision board to help you stay focused and motivated as you work toward these goals.

Anointing oils are a powerful tool that can be used with your vision board to help manifest your desires. Anointing oils are essential oils that are used in ritual and spiritual practices. They can anoint candles, crystals, or other objects that represent your desires, including your vision board.

Choose an anointing oil that resonates with your desires. For example, if you want to manifest prosperity, you may choose an oil that contains cinnamon or patchouli. Once you have chosen your oil, take a moment to meditate with it. Hold the bottle in your hands, close your eyes, and visualize your desires coming to fruition. Then, anoint your vision board with the oil, focusing your energy and intention on your desires as you do so.

I am healthy and strong, and my body is capable of healing itself

Crystals are powerful tools that can help to amplify your desires. They can enhance the energy of your vision board or you can carry the crystal with you as a reminder of your desires.

Choose a crystal that resonates with your desires.

Citrine is often used for manifesting abundance, while rose quartz is used for manifesting love and relationships.

Place a crystal grid around your vision board, glue crystals onto your board itself, or lay crystals along the top edge of the frame or corkboard if you have made a physical vision board.

If you have a digital vision board, you can carry the crystal with you.

Using Oracle Cards cards is a powerful tool that can help you gain insight and guidance on your manifestation journey. Oracle cards can help you connect with your intuition and to gain clarity on your desires.

Choose an Oracle deck that resonates with you. There are many decks available, so choose one that feels right to you.

Begin by shuffling your deck and asking for guidance on your desires. Then, draw a card and place it on your vision board. Consider the message of the card and how it relates to your desires. You may even want to write the message of the card on your board as a reminder of the guidance you have received. Take some time to meditate on your card and to reflect on its meaning. Use the guidance from your card to help you stay focused on your desires. You can also use oracle cards to ask specific questions about your desires and receive guidance on how to bring them into manifestation.

A vision board can be a powerful tool to help us focus our energy and bring our intentions to fruition. By using a vision board to visualize, set goals, and take action toward our desires, we can create the lives we truly want to live.

Finally, it's important to remember that manifestation is not just about visualizing and setting intentions - it's also about taking action toward your desires. Your vision board can help you stay focused and motivated, but it's up to you to take the steps necessary to bring your dreams into reality. Use your vision board as a tool to help you stay on track and keep your energy focused on your goals, but don't forget that you are the one who has the power to make things happen.

Spells for Abundance

A spell is an act of will and intention.

It's a way of harnessing the power of your mind, body, and spirit to create a desired outcome. Spells can bring about positive change in your life, from manifesting wealth and abundance to finding love and happiness. When you cast a spell, you're essentially calling on the universe to help you manifest your goal.

Casting spells for abundance can be a powerful way to manifest the life you want. With the right intention, focus, and determination, you can use spells to create an abundance of love, joy, and wealth in your life.

With casting spells for abundance, it's important to remember that the power of intention is key.

Before you cast a spell, take a few moments to consider what it is you truly desire. Write it down if you need to. Once you have a clear idea of what it is you want, you can begin to craft your spell.

When looking for a spell, it's important to find one that resonates with you and that you feel comfortable doing.

With casting a spell to bring abundance into your life, there are a few things to keep in mind.

First, consider what kind of abundance you want to bring into your life.

Do you want money?

Love?

Health?

Connection?

Then, choose a spell that best suits your needs.

There are many ways to cast spells for abundance. You might choose to use herbs, oils, runes, candles, and other tools to help you focus your energy and intentions. You can write your own spell, using words that express your desire and draw energy from the natural world.

Keep in mind that it's important to focus on your intention. The more focused and determined you are, the more powerful your spell will be. Remember to be patient, as it may take some time before you see results.

Casting a spell is simple.

You will need a few items, including a candle, a piece of paper, and a pen. Start by writing exactly what you need on the piece of paper. Be precise and state the exact amount of money you need and the timeline you need it in.

Speak your words with confidence, clarity, and a warm and friendly tone of voice. This will help to ensure that your spell is successful.

··•))●((•··

If you're looking for money and wealth, consider the Money Manifestation Spell. Casting a spell when you need money quickly can be surprisingly effective. Spells are a form of focused intent and can help you manifest money in an emergency.

When you cast a spell for money, you are connecting with the powers of the universe and asking for help.

Start by writing your intention on a piece of paper.

Take a few deep breaths and relax.

Visualize the money you need entering your life.

Feel the gratitude for the money being provided for you.

Then, light a green or gold candle and focus on the flame. Focus your energy on your intention while you concentrate on the flame.

Visualize yourself with abundance and feel the feelings of gratitude.

Then, take the paper you wrote your request on and hold it in your hands. Speak your intent out loud and recite the words of your spell. Ask the universe for the money you need and thank the universe for its help.

Finally, say the chant, "Money, come to me. I am deserving, I am worthy. I am open and ready to accept your abundance."

Repeat this chant as many times as you need to and then release the energy into the universe.

When you are done, blow out the candle and let the spell go. Trust that the universe will provide the money you need and that it will come to you at the right time.

··)) ● ((·

If you're looking for love, consider the Love Manifestation Spell.

Write your intention on a piece of paper.

Light a pink or red candle and focus your energy on your intention.

Visualize yourself with love and feel the feelings of joy.

Then, chant "Love, come to me. I am deserving, I am worthy. I am open and ready to accept your love."

Repeat this chant as many times as you need to and then release the energy into the universe.

··•)）●(（•··

Cord spells are simple and straightforward. All you need is a cord or ribbon, and your intentions. A cord spell is a simple and powerful magical ritual used to attract abundance and prosperity.

This spell involves tying knots in a length of cord or ribbon while chanting magical incantations. As we tie the knots, we charge the spell with the specific intent of bringing good luck and success in business and career.

To begin your cord spell, choose a length of ribbon or cord that is long enough to have at least three knots tied in it. Choose a ribbon or cord that has some kind of special significance to you, such as a color or material that resonates with you.

When performing the cord spell, chant words of your choosing or you can use one of the following spells.

"Knots of luck and success, bring me the wealth and gain I seek. Tied with intent and power, bring me fortune and prosperity."

"Good luck and success come to me. Strength and prosperity be mine. My business will thrive, so mote it be."

"I tie this cord for luck in my business and career. Bringing me success and abundance every year. As I tie this cord, my wishes come true. Bringing me luck that is sure to shine through."

As you chant, tie a knot in the cord or ribbon for each phrase.

As you tie each knot, focus on your intent and the energy of the chant. Feel the power of the spell being infused with your intent. When you have tied all the knots, tie the end of the ribbon in a secure knot to seal in the spell.

Then take a few moments to focus on your intent and the energy of the spell.

Visualize the outcome you desire and feel the energy of good luck and success flowing through you.

Once you have tied all the knots, tie the ends together and hang the cord or ribbon somewhere where it won't be disturbed. The power of this cord spell is that it helps to focus your energy and create an energy field around you that will help bring luck and success to your business and career. Leave it there until your wish is granted and the cord spell has been fulfilled.

You may also burn the cord or ribbon. As you do so, imagine the energy of the spell being released into the universe, bringing good luck and success into your business or career.

I am attracting opportunities that align with my purpose and passions

Crystals for Abundance

If you're looking to manifest wealth, love, and abundance in your life, crystals are a powerful tool to draw on. Crystals can help you gain clarity and focus, open up new opportunities, and attract energy, luck, and abundance so you can achieve your goals.

Crystals have the power to attract money, and abundance, and make your financial intentions stronger. There are lots of ways int incorporate crystals into your manifesting abundance practice.

*I let go of fear and
doubt and trust in the
universe to guide me
towards my desires*

Carrying pieces of crystals in your purse, pocket, or wallet can help you make good purchasing decisions throughout the day.

Place a group of crystals for abundance in the left-hand corner of your office or home. This will help bring prosperity and wealth your way.

Sleep with the crystals under your pillow in order to bring your abundance, love, and money-making ideas to you while you rest.

When visualizing your intention, place a crystal on its associated chakra. This will help you focus on your goals and make it easier to reach them.

You can also wear the crystals in pieces of jewelry in order to dispel any negative energy while attracting prosperity and wealth.

Using the crystals in your meditation is also an important step in achieving your financial goals. Focusing on abundance and wealth during your meditation will help you focus on your goals and make them a reality.

Place the crystals around your home to attract the energy of money and abundance. Place crystals such as citrine, pyrite, or green aventurine on your manifestation altar or carry them with you throughout the day. These crystals can help you attract abundance and prosperity into your life.

··•)) ● ((•··

You can also use crystals in your elixirs in order to harness our powerful energies. Creating an elixir with the right crystals can help to manifest your intentions in a powerful way.

To make an elixir using crystals for abundance, you will need to gather the following materials:

- A clear glass bottle or jar with a lid
- A small piece of citrine crystal
- A small piece of green aventurine crystal
- A small piece of pyrite crystal
- Filtered or spring water
- Essential oils such as patchouli or cinnamon. (optional)

Here are the steps to follow:

1. Cleanse your crystals by placing them in a bowl of sea salt or under running water. You can also cleanse the crystal by holding it under running water or smudging it with sage.

2. Fill your glass bottle or jar with filtered or spring water.

3. Add the citrine, green aventurine, and pyrite crystals to the water.

4. Close the lid of the bottle or jar and shake it gently to mix the ingredients together.

5. Place the bottle or jar in a sunny spot for several hours to allow the crystals to infuse with the water.

6. Once the water has been infused with the crystal's energy, remove the crystal. If it feels right to you, add a few drops of essential oil, such as patchouli or cinnamon, to the water. These oils promote abundance and prosperity.

Once the elixir is infused, use it to anoint yourself or objects for abundance. You can add it to your bath or use it in rituals to attract abundance into your life. Remember to set your intention and visualize your desired outcome as you consume the elixir.

Store your elixir in a cool, dry place and discard it after a few days.

My dream job is
manifesting for
me effortlessly
and easily

Let's take a closer look at how each crystal can help you on your journey to abundance and wealth.

Aventurine is often used by gamblers and brings optimism, opportunity, and luck. This crystal can also help you get back any money you regret having spent. It can also help you grasp opportunities that may have otherwise slipped your grasp.

Citrine is the stone of merchants. It is a powerful aid for all business owners and entrepreneurs. This crystal helps to soothe money anxiety and brings joy and optimism. It helps to encourage you to spend your money wisely, while also attracting luck and money into your life.

Rose quartz is a powerful crystal that has long been associated with love and romance. Witches use rose quartz to attract love into our lives or to strengthen existing relationships. The energy of rose quartz is known for its ability to open the heart chakra, which is the center of love and compassion. By using rose quartz in your practice, you can tap into this energy and use it to manifest your desires. When working with rose quartz, use it in meditation, carry it with you, or place it on your altar. You may also incorporate it into love spells or rituals. The gentle, soothing energy of rose quartz can help to reduce stress and anxiety, which can make it easier to attract and maintain healthy relationships.

Tiger Eye is the crystal of motivation and confidence and brings luck and abundance into your life. It can help you see situations with a fresh perspective and bring your dreams to reality. It's an excellent stone to keep close when you are starting a new business. Tiger Eye is also said to give you the willpower of the tiger, so you can face any fear with confidence.

Amethyst is a crystal that draws wealth. It encourages you to believe in your worthiness and creates an environment that attracts abundance and money into your life. Its calming and soothing vibrations remove doubts and fears in terms of investments and career decisions.

Pyrite is a powerful stone that helps you attract wealth, encourages success, and shields against negative energies. It's the perfect crystal to have if you're a financial advisor, as it helps you make wise decisions and helps your clients make our money grow.

Moss agate is a stone of stability and new beginnings, perfect for those wanting to create financial success and stability for themselves. It has a soothing energy that helps you improve your self-esteem, which is key for success.

Jade is the "stone of wealth and success". It's an extremely lucky stone that helps dissolve self-imposed limitations, particularly the ones related to not being worthy of receiving abundance and money. Jade encourages wisdom and harmony, and helps you make crucial decisions about using and investing your money. It also protects you from disasters.

Clear Quartz is a powerful crystal that amplifies energy. Reach for your clear quarts when you are looking to bring abundance, harmony, love, vitality, and prosperity into your life. It can also help to cleanse and purify the emotional body.

Malachite is a stone of energy. Use malachite to help manifest your financial goals. Placing this crystal with money can help to give you focus and solve any financial issues you may be facing. It also has the power to give you an unshakeable confidence and courage to take risks in making financial decisions.

Amazonite is the stone of hope and is great for helping you to realize your dreams and bring abundance into your life. Amazonite dissipates energy blockages and helps to bring positive emotions to any financial venture. It also can help to bring courage to take risks in creating something new, as well as clearing away any negative feelings that may hold you back from achieving your dreams. Finally, it can help to calm your mind during stressful work situations.

Labradorite is a powerful crystal that clears your mind, protects you from making poor decisions, increases your self-confidence, and boosts your creativity. The perfect crystal to help you when you feel stuck in life. Labradorite is known as the wealth and money stone, and can help you draw abundance and prosperity into your life.

Peridot is an ideal stone when you're looking to increase your wealth. Its energy helps to eliminate negative self-beliefs that hinder your ability to attract and maintain greater wealth. Peridot also helps to make you feel worthy of receiving abundance and money, which in turn helps to boost the desired situation.

Garnet is a fantastic crystal for manifesting dreams and ideas. It has a powerful energy that helps to turn your visions into reality and encourages self-improvement related to abundance and prosperity. Garnet also blocks out the negative energy that drains your luck in wealth. With its positive energy, Garnet helps to attract luck, abundance, and opportunities. It can also help you advance the career ladder and create new business relationships.

Finally, Shungite is a money magnet stone, and is perfect for helping you to attract positivity, good luck, and abundance into your life. Its energy helps to repel negative energy and attract positive energy, while also helping to keep your finances in check.

No matter your financial goals, these stones can help to bring you closer to your dreams. Working with them can help to attract wealth and abundance, while also protecting you from negative energies. With the help of these crystals, you can be sure of achieving your financial goals. From boosting your confidence to creating positive energy and providing emotional support, these stones are a great aid to achieving the financial stability you're looking for.

So if you're looking to make your money grow, bring love and success into your life, while connecting to your intuition, there is a stone that is the perfect addition to your journey.

Ritual Oils for Abundance

Traditional ritual oils have been used for centuries to help bring good fortune, wealth, and abundance into our lives. They are an integral part of many spiritual practices and have been used to help with love, luck, and prosperity.

The oils are usually made with a base oil, essential oils, herbs, or other ingredients. Each ingredient has its own unique properties and meaning, so it's important to choose the right combination for your ritual.

Ritual oils are a blend of natural ingredients that have been carefully chosen based on our energy and ability to attract positive energy. The principal ingredients are natural herbs, roots, and resins. Together, they create a powerful combination that can help draw in more money, abundance, success, and prosperity.

The way the oil works is that it contains the magnetic energy of abundance. When the oil is applied to the body, it helps to create a powerful vibration that attracts money and prosperity. This vibration can help to open up pathways to financial success and abundance.

Your oil can be used to anoint yourself, and your space, and to bless any items you may use in your ritual practice. You can also infuse your ritual oils with your intention and use them in spells, charms, and other magickal workings.

Good options for a base oil include Jojoba, Coconut, and Olive oil. These are all good options for our moisturizing and nourishing properties.

The next step is to choose the right essential oils for your ritual oil.

Essential oils are powerful tools that can achieve a variety of desired effects. Some of the best essential oils for abundance and prosperity include orange, jasmine, lavender, cedarwood, clove, frankincense, rosemary, sandalwood and bergamot.

It's also important to choose an oil that resonates with you. This will make it easier to connect with your intention and call in the energy of abundance and prosperity. It's also important to use high-quality oils when possible, as they will be more effective at manifesting your intentions.

The last step is to choose the right herbs or other ingredients. This can include a variety of herbs such as basil, thyme, or Sage. You can also add additional ingredients such as crystals or dried flowers to your ritual oil.

Now that you know the basics, let's talk about how to craft your own ritual oil for abundance and prosperity.

First, start by pouring your base oil into a glass jar. Then add your chosen essential oils and herbs. Finally, add any additional ingredients to the jar. Mix the ingredients together thoroughly.

Once all of your ingredients are combined, you can then close the jar and let the oil sit for at least a week. This will give the ingredients time to blend and create a powerful ritual oil.

Some examples of ritual oils are:

···)) ● (((···

Money Drawing Oil

This oil is traditionally used to draw in more money and prosperity into your life. Money drawing oil can help open up pathways to financial abundance. It's made from a mixture of herbs, roots, and flowers that are believed to attract wealth and abundance, including clove, cinnamon, and nutmeg. Anoint yourself with it before you embark on your next business venture or use it to anoint coins, bills, and other money symbols in order to increase our power of attraction.

Abundance Oil

This oil helps you manifest abundance in all areas of your life. It's usually made with a combination of herbs and flowers that symbolize abundance and prosperity. We start with a base of jojoba oil and then add a blend of essential oils such as orange, patchouli, and juniper berry. When combined, these essential oils open the heart, awaken creativity, and invoke a sense of abundance. When you use Abundance Oil, you'll be inspired to focus on your goals and dreams. The scent of the oil will remind you of the abundance that you can achieve.

Success Oil

This oil is used to bring success in any endeavor. It's usually made with herbs and spices that are believed to bring good luck and success. We can use Success Oil for a variety of purposes, such as job interviews, exams, business meetings, and even sports. It can help you stay focused and motivated, and help to bring success in all your endeavors. Success oil brings harmony and balance to the body and mind. It can reduce stress, anxiety, depression, help with concentration, focus, and mental clarity. Success oil is made using herbs and spices, such as cumin, bay leaves, turmeric, and other ingredients that are believed to bring good luck and success. Using success oil is easy. Simply light the oil over a flame and let the smoke drift through the air. As the smoke wafts through the air, it takes your hopes and dreams with it, seeking success and good luck in all that you do. The smoke carries with it the power of the herbs and spices, bringing with it all the good luck and success you need.

Prosperity Oil

This oil brings good luck, abundance, and prosperity into your life. It's made with a blend of herbs, roots, and flowers that symbolize abundance and prosperity. The herbs and roots used in this oil give you just the right blessing of good luck and abundance, cedar and sage to purify and protect, bay leaf and allspice to bring wealth and good fortune, lavender and rose to bring beauty, love, and joy into your life. Prosperity Oil is easy to use.

All you need to do is take a few drops of the oil and apply it to your skin or clothing. As you rub it in, you'll feel the energy of prosperity and abundance entering your life. You can also add a few drops to a diffuser to bring the scent of prosperity into your home or office.

Now you're ready to use your ritual oil for abundance and prosperity.

To use it, simply dab a small amount of the oil onto your wrists and forehead and then meditate for a few minutes. You can also use your oils to annoint your vision board, candles and other meaningful things. These oils will help to bring good luck, wealth, and abundance into your life.

Keep them in a safe place, out of the reach of children, pets, and other animals.

Manifesting and the Moon

T he moon has an ability to influence our lives. The phases of the moon are a guide to harnessing its energy and using it to manifest abundance in our lives.

The moon has been revered for its power and influence since ancient times. Its gravitational pull affects the tides, the growth of plants, and even our own bodies.

By syncing your intentions and rituals with the lunar cycle, you can tap into the energy of the universe and attract abundance in all forms.

The moon goes through a cycle of eight phases, each with its own unique energy and symbolism.

The moon has two main phases that are especially important for manifestation: the new moon and the full moon.

The new moon is the first phase of the cycle, and it represents new beginnings and fresh starts. The new moon is the beginning of the lunar cycle, and it's the perfect time to set your intentions for the month ahead.

The full moon is the peak of the lunar cycle, and it's the ideal time to release any limiting beliefs or negative energy that may block your abundance.

Before you begin any ritual or intention-setting, it's essential to clear your space of any negative energy. You can do this by smudging with sage, palo santo, or any other cleansing herb of your choice. You can also use crystals or essential oils to purify your space.

Sit in a quiet, comfortable place and take a few deep breaths to center yourself. You can also meditate or do some gentle yoga to help you connect with your inner self.

Write down your fears, doubts, or limiting beliefs, and then burn them in a fire or bury them in the earth.

Write down your intentions for the month ahead. Be specific and use positive language. For example, instead of saying, "I want to be debt-free," say, "I am abundant and financially free."

If you use crystals in your practice, you can charge them with your intentions by placing them in the light of the new moon. You can also hold them in your hands and visualize your intentions flowing into them.

As the moon begins to wax and grow in size, continue to focus on your intentions and take action toward manifesting them. This might involve making changes in your daily routine, reaching out to potential opportunities, or simply staying open to receiving abundance in all its forms.

The full moon is the perfect time to release any negative energy or limiting beliefs that may block your abundance. Just like on the new moon, it's essential to clear your space of any negative energy before you begin your ritual.

You can use the same methods as before, or you can try something new.

Sit in a quiet, comfortable place and take a few deep breaths to center yourself. You can also meditate or do some gentle yoga to help you connect with your inner self.

Take a piece of paper and write down any limiting beliefs or negative energy that you want to release. Be specific and honest with yourself. This is your chance to let go of what's holding you back.

Once you've written down what you want to release, take the paper outside and burn it. As you watch the paper burn, visualize the negative energy or limiting beliefs leaving your life.

You can also recite a mantra or affirmation to help you release.

As you release these negative energies, focus on the abundance that you want to manifest in your life. Visualize yourself as a magnet for prosperity and feel the emotions of joy, gratitude, and abundance flowing through you.

If you use crystals in your practice, you can charge them with the energy of the full moon by placing them in the moon's light. You can also hold them in your hands and visualize the negative energy leaving your body and flowing into the crystals.

Working with the phases of the moon is a powerful way to manifest abundance in your life. By

setting your intentions on the new moon and releasing negative energy on the full moon, you can
tap into the energy of the universe and attract
abundance in all forms. Remember to stay positive,
be specific about your intentions, and trust in the
process. The universe has your back, and abundance is your birthright.

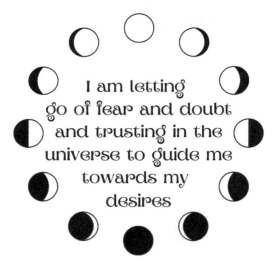

I am letting
go of fear and doubt
and trusting in the
universe to guide me
towards my
desires

Live As If

While there are many techniques and practices that can help us achieve our goals, one method that may surprise you is living your life as if you have already manifested your dreams.

This may sound counterintuitive, but it can actually be a powerful tool for creating the life you desire.

So, what exactly does it mean to live your life as if your dreams have already manifested?

Essentially, it means embodying the feelings and emotions you would have if your desires had already come true. It means acting as if you already have the job, the relationship, the abundance, or whatever you are seeking.

This can be challenging at first, but with practice, it becomes easier and can have a profound impact on your life.

One way that living as if your dreams have already manifested can help bring them into reality is by shifting your mindset. When you act as if your desires have already come true, you are signaling to the universe that you are ready and open to receive them. This can help to attract the people, opportunities, and resources that you need to make your dreams a reality.

For example, let's say that you are seeking a new job. Instead of constantly worrying about finding the perfect position, start living as if you have already landed the job of your dreams. This might mean updating your resume, networking with people in your desired industry, and dressing as if you were already working in that field. By embodying the feelings of success and abundance, you are signaling to the universe that you are ready to receive the job you desire.

Another way that living as if your dreams have already manifested can help is by helping you to stay focused on your goals. When you act as if your desires have already come true, you are less likely to get discouraged or give up on your dreams. You are more likely to stay motivated and take actions that will help you move closer to your goals.

For example, let's say that you are seeking to manifest a loving relationship. Instead of constantly worrying about being single or feeling lonely, start living as if you are already in a happy and fulfilling relationship.

This might mean setting aside time each day to visualize yourself in a happy relationship, practicing self-care, and engaging in activities that bring you joy. Buy yourself flowers, takes yourself on dates, and do things that make you happy.

By living as if your desires have already come true, you are more likely to attract a partner who aligns with your values and desires.

This doesn't mean lying to yourself or pretending that you're in a relationship when you're not. Rather, it means embodying the energy of love and partnership in your daily life. Dress up, go out, and socialize as if you're already in a happy relationship.

This energy will attract like-minded people into your life and put you in a better position to find the love you're looking for.

If your dream is to achieve financial abundance, start living your life as if you're already wealthy. This doesn't mean spending money you don't have or living beyond your means. Rather, it means cultivating a mindset of abundance and gratitude. Take care of yourself, invest in your own growth and well-being, and be generous with what you have. This energy will attract more abundance into your life and help you achieve the financial success you're looking for.

You can also write yourself a check for the amount of money you want. Seeing your desired amount written down will help you feel more connected to the goal. Put it somewhere where you'll see it every day, like a vision board, and let it be a reminder of what you're working toward. Believe that you can receive that amount of money and trust that the universe will respond to your desires.

Another way to live 'as if' is to pretend that each day you get money deposited into your account and have to spend it all.

How much money would be deposited?

What would you do with this money?

What would you buy?

What experiences would you have?

Visualize yourself enjoying these experiences and having all the money to do so.

If your dream is to achieve success in your career, start living your life as if you're already there. This doesn't mean quitting your job or acting arrogant. Rather, it means embodying the energy of success in everything you do. Dress for success, act with confidence and professionalism, and focus on building valuable relationships in your industry. This energy will attract opportunities and success into your life and help you achieve your career goals.

Do you have a dream home you want to manifest in your life? Look at real estate websites to find your dream home. Tour the home in your mind or at an open house. How would it be to live there? Visualize yourself living in the home, walking through the rooms, and imagining where you would put your clothes, your shoes, and how you would cook meals in the kitchen. Get excited about what it would be like to own that home and live your life as if it were already yours.

If you dream of traveling, watch videos or make idea boards for your dream trip. Imagine the trip as if you are there now. Feel the sun on your skin. Imagine the salty water. Smell the pine air of the forest as you hike up the mountain.

You can do this with anything you deeply desire.

Living your life as if your dreams have already manifested can be a powerful tool for manifesting your desires as a witch. By embodying the feelings and emotions you would have if your dreams had already come true, you are signaling to the universe that you are ready and open to receive them. This can help to attract the people, opportunities, and resources that you need to make your dreams a reality. So, if you are seeking to manifest your desires, try living as if they have already come true and see what magic unfolds in your life.

You can also cast a spell for abundance. This is an ancient practice that has been used for millennia to manifest wealth, health, and happiness. You can use your own words to create a powerful spell or use words from a trusted source. Focus on the feeling of abundance that you want to manifest and be mindful of the words you choose.

···)) ● (((···

Live as if....

Before we get started, take a few moments to relax your body and mind. Sit in a comfortable position and allow your breathing to become slow and steady.

Repeat this sentence to yourself: "I am willing to receive. Money flows to me with ease. My time is coming."

Take a few moments to really feel these words before repeating them. As you say them, allow yourself to open up to the possibility of receiving money with ease.

"I am willing to receive" is about allowing yourself to receive all the good that is coming your way. It's about being open to the abundance that is available to you. It's about allowing the Universe to provide for you.

Money can be a positive force in your life. Release any negative beliefs you may have about money, and trust that you can attract and receive it.

Visualize a river of money flowing toward you.

Imagine how it feels to receive the money.

Let yourself be open to the abundance that is coming your way.

"My time is coming". This is a reminder that the Universe has your back and that whatever you desire is coming your way. You can manifest whatever you want. You have the power to create the life you desire.

Now acknowledge the feelings of abundance and gratitude within you.

Feel the joy of receiving money with ease.

Now let yourself return to a state of relaxation. Let go of thoughts and worries and just be.

Take a few moments to bask in this feeling before returning to your normal state of being. When you're ready, open your eyes and take a few moments to reflect on how you feel.

The universe
is conspiring
to bring me all the
abundance
I desire

Take Inspired Action

One of the biggest misconceptions about manifestation is that it is solely about setting intentions and waiting for them to magically come to fruition. In reality, manifestation requires a combination of both intention and action. Taking inspired action toward your goals each day is crucial to manifesting the life you desire.

When you take action toward your desires, you are actively aligning yourself with the energy of abundance and attracting more opportunities for success.

Whether it's making a phone call, sending an email, or taking a class to improve your skills, any step you take toward your goals is a step in the right direction.

One of the most important things to remember when taking inspired action is to keep your intentions in mind. This means staying focused on your goals and taking actions that are in alignment with them. Write your goals and be specific about what you want to manifest. This will help you stay focused and motivated as you take action toward your goals.

For example, if your goal is to start your own business, taking a class on entrepreneurship or reaching out to potential investors would be actions that are in alignment with that goal.

Once you have set your goals, create a plan of action. Break your goals down into smaller, more manageable steps.

This will make them seem less overwhelming and help you stay motivated.

Write each step and give yourself a deadline for completing them. This will help you stay on track and ensure that you are making progress toward your goals each day.

Another important aspect of taking inspired action is to stay open to new opportunities. Sometimes the action you need to take may not be immediately apparent, but by remaining open to new opportunities and experiences, you may stumble upon the perfect action to take toward your goals. This could be something as simple as attending a networking event or striking up a conversation with a stranger who happens to be in the same field as you.

Sometimes our goals can feel overwhelming, especially if they're big or long-term. To make them more manageable, break them down into smaller, achievable steps. This will make it easier to take action each day and keep moving toward your goals. It's also important to remember that taking action toward your goals doesn't have to be a daunting task. Small actions taken consistently can add up to big results over time. For example, if your goal is to write a book, committing to writing just 500 words a day can turn into a completed manuscript in just a few months.

Consistency is key when it comes to manifestation. Make a commitment to take action toward your goals every day, no matter how small it may seem. This will help you build momentum and stay aligned with the energy of abundance.

Taking inspired action toward your goals may require you to step out of your comfort zone. Embrace change and be willing to try new things. This will help you grow and expand your horizons.

Visualizing yourself already, achieving your goals, and affirming positive statements to yourself can help to shift your mindset and attract more abundance into your life. This positive energy can then fuel your inspired actions and help you achieve your goals even faster.

By taking action toward your goals, you align yourself with the energy of abundance and attract more opportunities for success.

Manifestation is not always a linear journey. There may be setbacks or obstacles along the way, but it's important to trust the process and keep taking action toward your goals. Remember that every step you take is bringing you closer to manifesting your desires.

By staying focused on your goals, staying open to new opportunities, and committing to taking small actions consistently, you can align yourself with the energy of abundance and attract more opportunities for success into your life.

Celebrate Successes

It's easy to get caught up in the hustle and bustle of our daily lives, constantly pushing ourselves to achieve more and reach for bigger successes.

But sometimes, it's important to take a step back and appreciate the abundance and successes we have already manifested in our lives. No matter how big or small, each success is a stepping stone toward creating the life we desire.

By celebrating our successes, we cultivate feelings of gratitude and abundance. These positive emotions can help us keep our momentum going and continue moving in the right direction. When we focus on the successes we've already achieved, we create a positive mindset and attract more abundance and success into our lives.

You don't need to wait for an enormous success to appreciate the little ones.

We can celebrate the abundance in the small moments, such as a peaceful morning, a beautiful sunset, or a delicious meal. Or maybe you landed your dream job, manifested a new love interest, or simply had a great day. Whatever it may be, take the time to acknowledge and celebrate it.

So take a moment to pause and reflect on all the successes and abundance you have already created in your life. Allow yourself to bask in the joy of achieving your goals and dreams, no matter how big or small.

You can celebrate your successes in many ways.

You might write them down in a journal, light a candle and meditate on them, or simply take a moment to express gratitude for them.

Thank yourself for your successes. Acknowledge all the hard work and effort that you have put into achieving your goals and dreams. Feel the pride and joy that comes with each accomplishment.

Think of a goal that you have achieved and take a moment to feel proud of yourself.

If you can, remember a feeling you experienced when you manifested the success. Maybe it was relief, joy, pride, or a combination of emotions.

Allow yourself to celebrate the success and the emotions it brings.

Now, bring your focus to the present.

How has achieving this goal impacted your life?

Take a moment to appreciate the way your success has positively affected your life.

Now, think of another success you have achieved.

Take a moment to recognize the hard work and dedication it took to manifest that success. Again, take a moment to celebrate the success and the emotions it brings.

Now, bring your focus to the present.

How has achieving this goal affected your life?

Take a moment to appreciate the way your success has positively affected your life.

Continue this process until you have gone through all of your successes.

Now think of the successes that you are manifesting in your life right now. All the hard work and effort that you are putting into achieving your goals. Feel the joy and satisfaction that comes with striving for something and achieving it.

Finally, think of the successes that you will manifest in the future. Visualize the goals that you want to accomplish and feel the motivation and excitement that comes with working toward them.

Take a few moments to relish in all the successes that you have manifested in your life. Allow yourself to feel the joy and satisfaction that comes with achieving your goals. Celebrate your successes and enjoy the feeling of accomplishment.

Allow yourself to feel the pride, joy, and satisfaction that each success has brought you. Remind yourself that you are capable and strong, and that anything you set your mind to is achievable with enough dedication and hard work.

Now, repeat the following affirmation to yourself: "I am proud of my accomplishments and I am worthy of celebrating my successes."

Whatever method you choose, make sure you take the time to truly feel the emotions of gratitude and abundance. As witches, we have the power to create the life we desire. By celebrating our successes and cultivating positive emotions, we can continue to manifest abundance and success in our lives.

Remember that each success is an opportunity to grow and create a life you love. Take this feeling of pride and accomplishment with you throughout your day.

⋯•)）●（(•⋯

To celebrate your successes in manifesting abundance in your life, you can perform a ritual to honor the universe and express gratitude.

Here's a simple ritual you can follow:

Find a quiet and comfortable place where you won't be disturbed. Light some candles, burn incense or sage, and set up your altar with crystals, symbols, or anything that resonates with you.

Take a few deep breaths and visualize roots growing from your feet, connecting you to the earth. Feel the energy of the earth grounding you and helping you stay centered.

Take a moment to reflect on all the successes you've achieved in manifesting abundance in your life. Think of all the positive changes, opportunities, and abundance that have come your way.

Express your gratitude to the universe, the elements, the spirits, and all the beings that have helped you along the way. You can say a prayer, chant a mantra, or simply speak from your heart.

As an offering of gratitude, you can offer a gift to the universe, such as a crystal, a flower, or anything that represents your appreciation.

When you feel complete, thank the universe, the elements, the spirits, and all the beings that have been with you during the ritual. Release the energy and close your sacred space. Remember, the most important part of any ritual is your intention and your connection to your inner self and the universe. Trust your intuition and let the ritual flow naturally. May your life be filled with abundance that continues to grow with each passing day.

Made in United States
Troutdale, OR
11/07/2023

14360538R00086